Brigh

Here's to
growing
friendships!

Enjoy the book!

Love you guys!

~She GarC

LIFE AS SHE DOES IT PRESENTS:

A LIFE OF
flavor

SHEILA M. GARCIA

LUCIDBOOKS

*A book about finding joy in life's hard times,
with matching recipes to comfort you.*

*I dedicate this book to the family and friends that have
always had my back, through the good times and the bad,
and who have been there in my greatest times of need.
And to those who love and enjoy my food.
You know who you are.*

Contents

Prologue

There are times when you feel that everything is perfect, when everything seems to be in place—your job, your marriage and relationships, your community—everything. And if you're anything like I used to be, you just wait for the proverbial anvil to fall from the sky.

I have seen some hard times: the kind of hard times that put all the good times on the back shelf of our hearts. And I mean some hard times! Our house has been struck by lightning—and so have I! I've broken just about every bone in my body at one time or another. The Hubster and I have lost our jobs, sometimes at the same time, on several occasions. Our son was diagnosed with a terrible, chronic, and debilitating disease. My car caught on fire while I was driving it. I'm telling you, People, the list goes on and on and on.

These are things that happen in life though—illness, death, job loss, disease, unhealthy relationships. And we, as mere mortals, tend to cling to those problems, holding them close to the vest and wondering, "Why me?"

And doesn't every one of those things mentioned, and then some, revolve around food? When someone is sick, you make chicken soup or bring a meal. When a community member loses a job, someone starts a meal train. When there is a breakup, that pint of ice cream is the immediate reaction.

Think about it: weddings, we eat; graduations, we eat; funerals, we eat; celebrations, we eat; first dates, and most dates, we eat; sadness, happiness, provision—we eat! I fancy myself a rather respectable "cooker" (as my youngest son once called me) and a large contributor to the foodie continuum, which helps during the times mentioned above.

Through some experience, lots of faith, and tons of food, I have learned that hard times are a part of life, and they don't make life bad. Hard times mean we have been given a huge responsibility to value and respect this one life we've been given, through the good and the not-so-good. In this book you will find a few tales from my story of how I found the inspiration to move forward. Each story is followed by a recipe that comforted and inspired me along the way. It's my own life, love, and food story. I hope it inspires you to move forward in your own story as well.

RECIPE
for Disaster

I am married to my best friend. So cliché, I know. But as much as I don't like to conform, I don't mind this cliché so much because it's so true. But that wasn't always the case, Readers. I struggled in an unhealthy and beyond-dysfunctional first marriage for nine years of my life.

How'd that go down? How do first marriages often go down? I'd like to say we were young and in love—us against the world, and we made an immature decision to get married, throwing caution to the wind. That would make the story a bit wonderful, wouldn't it? The truth is, we met through the party scene. We had mutual friends, so we hung out, partying.

I take full responsibility for my part in this next piece of the puzzle; I could have easily said no. And when I say, "Just say no," I am not referring to the slogan we all know it to be. Let me explain.

One day we were over at his mother's house when she suggested we should get married. We looked at each other and laughed. She suggested it again. We laughed again. She said, "Follow me." And we blindly did. We were led into a bedroom where she motioned us to sit down on the bed. She backed up to the door and said, "You're

1

not allowed to come out until you've set a date." And she walked out and left us alone.

So we sat there, looking at each other, just wanting to go party some more but knowing his mom was serious. Looking back on it, it was almost like a double-dog dare, and I was certainly not one to back down from a dare or challenge.

He looked at me and said, "Well, I suppose if I get married to anyone, it would be you."

Be still, my heart! So I said, "Fine. Two years. We will wait two years." The romance in the air was palpable as we shook on it.

As we filed out of the room ready to set our parameters and give his mother the scoop, she said, "It needs to be on your grandmother's birthday! She will LOVE that! No *if*s, *and*s, or *but*s. Let's call her and tell her!"

His grandmother's birthday was a month away. Oh, did I mention we had been hanging out for only two months? We knew absolutely nothing about one another. We had been partying together for two months, and it was one month before the grandmother's birthday. That equals three months of being around one another before wedded bliss begins. Sure, why not?

Oh, and it was lovely. This was in the early 90s, so the poufy wedding dress sleeves were a big hit as we exchanged vows (oh geez) under his grandparents' gazebo. Since we are set in the appropriate era for it, picture Wayne and Garth from *Wayne's World* wiggling their fingers: *doodle-loodle-loot! Doodle-loodle-loot!*

Before the wedding, shortly before we exchanged a near decade of insanity, I sat down and asked those in the room to "pray" with me. I had no idea what that meant; I just thought it was something I was supposed to say. I closed my eyes and clasped my hands together in my lap and sat there in silence. I was thinking about how the night before I had told a friend I could "learn to love him, I'm sure." I thought about the string of horrific events that had happened in my life (aka, the frying pan), and how I somehow knew in my heart the horrific events that lay before me (the fire). I then raised my head and did the sign of the cross as I had seen people do before, and said "ahh-men." And I walked that green mile.

From that moment until the moment my marriage dissolved, things took place between us that no one would call bliss. We shared bad times and worse times—things I can only allow your imagination to create for the sake of my family.

How does this chapter end with such a recipe for disaster from the start? With nine years of two people living in solitary misery, with me trying to fill a void in my heart with more bad decisions, violence, and a sinister power that could destroy a person emotionally.

But the glimmer during that time was that I found my faith—or rather, it found me. I also gave birth to two marvelous humans, which makes me know I wouldn't trade the dreadfulness of that union for anything, even if I could. And that recipe for disaster gave me glimmers of hope for what was to come.

Are you looking for the potential glimmer in the hardest moments? Are you overlooking what is right before your eyes? Don't jump from the frying pan and into the fire, at least not on purpose. We as flawed humans make mistakes—over and over again. We fail and then get angry at what our lives have turned out to be, blaming others and letting it take us out emotionally. What is the good that has come from the bad? What kind of tasty delight can you make from a recipe for disaster?

RECIPE FOR DISASTER CHOCOLATE AVOCADO GLIMMERS

6 oz dark chocolate
1 small-to-medium avocado
3/4 tsp vanilla extract
1/8 tsp sea salt
cocoa powder and edible glitter, to roll your truffles

Combine the chocolate, vanilla extract, and sea salt over a double boiler. Melt until completely smooth. I don't have a double boiler, so I use a tempered-glass or oven-safe bowl over a small pot or pan. Mash the avocado until smooth, and then stir it into the melted chocolate mixture until thick. Put the bowl into your refrigerator for about 15–20 minutes, or until the mixture is firm to the touch.

When the chocolate-avocado mixture has firmed up, use a melon baller or ice cream scoop to make uniform balls. Roll the balls between the palms of your hand until smooth and place onto wax or parchment paper. If it gets a little messy as you go, place the bowl back in the fridge for a few minutes to firm the mixture back up.

On a separate plate or bowl, blend cocoa powder and edible glitter, and roll each truffle to coat. Serve immediately or store in the fridge until ready to serve.

No frying pan; no fire. At first glance, this seems like a very bad combination—like a recipe for disaster—but if you have faith and bite into it, it turns out to be a tasty delight!

THE
Perfect Blend

When I met Adrian (aka "The Hubster"), it was clear we had similar baggage. We both came from a not-so-amicable divorce, we both had children from that previous marriage, and we both were never going to get married again. (You see how that worked out.)

These days, we live in a society of blended families. It's the norm, really. People never used to be as surprised to hear an older, married couple say they were celebrating their 25th, 40th, or 50th wedding anniversary. Nowadays, it's astonishing just to hear if someone hasn't been divorced at least once—and I'm part of that society.

After we started seeing each other on a serious level (sounds so mature, doesn't it?), we knew that we weren't seeing just each other, but also each other's children. Then, when we got married, we knew we weren't marrying just each other, but becoming part of the parental unit the children would share. As a person of faith, I can tell you that the moment I accepted Adrian's proposal, I prayed he would be an example of a man that would buy the truth and not sell it; gain wisdom, instruction, and understanding; and then deliver it to our children. I prayed with all my might he would put aside all judgment and generously share with the children his unconditional love he had for me, and that he would have a "Joseph spirit" (Joseph, the stepfather of Jesus, who in my opinion was the greatest stepfather who ever lived).

I prayed he would be the perfect father, and that together we would be the perfect parents.

(Naïve, right?) I now consider myself the richest woman in the world because of my full heart, but such love has not come without its trials, pitfalls, difficulties, and snags. The process has been less-than-perfect. There have been disagreements, arguments, knock-down-drag-outs, and moments we are less than proud of. We have seen illness, death, valleys, and psychiatrists. We have had seasons of gaining friends and family, but also seasons of losing. We have shared in drama, defeat, lost savings; had powerful, emotional lows; and scraped the bottom of life's barrel. And we did it all together.

Don't get me wrong: all of us—Adrian, me, and the kids—have worked at it with all our hearts, and the price of the success we share as a family unit came through that hard work and dedication. With all of those things, we have also seen grace, mercy, compassion, and triumph over illness. We have been taught endurance; we've grown in faith, strength, and perseverance; and we've learned to trust. We have celebrated the peaks, marriages, each other, life, and love. And we did it all together.

We have a beautiful family, and we are protective of that. We live a charmed life, always trying to enjoy the things that most people don't see right in front of them, and we are joyful and thankful for that. But if it was all taken away from us tomorrow—and it very well could be—we would remember life is a big canvas and we threw all the paint on it we could; we would remember we made the decision to be a family and commit ourselves to making it a success; we would remember that without the valleys there would be no peaks. We would remember we were given the gift of being like a unique wine—the gift of being intricately perfected and blended.

THE PERFECT BLEND STEW

2 tbs coconut flour
1 tsp sea salt
1 tsp pepper
1 tbs garlic powder
1 tbs cumin
1 tbs paprika
2 lbs beef stew meat
2 tbs butter
4 tbs canola oil
3 large carrots, washed and sliced
1 small pkg (8 oz) baby portabella mushrooms, sliced
2 cloves garlic, minced
1 onion, diced
1 1/2 cups beef broth
2 1/2 cups of your favorite red wine blend

Combine coconut flour and seasonings in a bowl, and then dredge your stew meat, coating completely in the seasoned flour mixture. Melt butter and oil in a heavy pot (I use my cast-iron Dutch oven!) and let it heat for a couple of minutes. Add the meat. Cook over medium-high heat, stirring occasionally, until meat is browned on all sides.

Add carrots, mushrooms, garlic, onion, beef broth, and wine. Bring to a boil, reduce heat to low, and cover, stirring occasionally for about two hours on low heat, or until meat is tender. Serve over jasmine rice, egg noodles, or as its own banquet in a bowl!

It doesn't matter what blend you use in the recipe. What matters is the flavor you add during the cooking process!

MY
First True Love

When I found out I was pregnant with my first child, my daughter Chelsea, I was beside myself with joy. My life up to that point was a roller coaster of ups and downs and downs and downs. With my failing marriage and emotional turmoil, this baby gave me hope I would finally have someone to love—to really, really love—and who would really, really love me.

The search for love had been long and hard. I'd spent 21 long years looking for a way to fill the void I'd always felt in my heart. I didn't know why the void was there, but I knew I needed to fill it. Now, I know this is not a practical or efficient way of thinking when it comes to bringing a human into the world, but I was not a practical thinker back then.

You've probably heard those stories of women who get pregnant but have no idea, and then have a tummy ache one day about nine months later and a baby pops out. That was not me. I believe I knew the very second I conceived this child. I felt a difference within me, down to my very soul. I had no concept of God and did not know (or care about) the meaning of life or the purpose of mine until that moment.

I couldn't wait for her to get here, to make her debut. Isn't it funny how we say we want a "baby?" We never consider the aches and pains of potty training, scrapes and bruises, and teenage years. We don't think about the fears and anxieties that go along with the first day of school, crossing the street, or the evil that exists in the world. We never hear anyone say, "I really want to have a wedding to pay for," or "We've been trying to have a college student." We always say, "I really want a baby," or "We've been trying to have a baby." And all I knew was I wanted this baby.

This is not a warm and fuzzy story though. Throughout the duration of my pregnancy, I gained a person. I don't mean the tiny person growing in my belly; I mean I gained about 15 pounds a month, which equates to approximately 120 pounds in nine months. This made me unhealthy and eventually bedridden. I was depressed about the life I had outside the safety of the belly, and scared to bring the life inside me into my world. But I focused on the pure love within me; I knew I was in the presence of greatness whenever she kicked, and that gave me hope. I actually get chills along my spine when I think about it to this day.

And then she arrived. Chelsea came into this world, and my heart exploded. I had spent my entire life looking for my true love. I looked high and low, even made it up as I went sometimes, only to discover I had been fooling myself in the long run.

But here was this person who had to do nothing to prove herself to me, whom I found myself connected to in a way I had never known before. She was my first true love. At that point, I had no relationship with God, yet I found myself thanking Him over and over again as I held Chelsea in my arms. I found myself praying for Him to protect her from harm, disease, and evil.

That little girl is now a mommy herself. She is awesome at motherhood, already way better than I ever was.

She was the first of many true loves to come into my life, for I had more children and a husband who rode in on a white horse and swept me off my feet. I also discovered along the way I had been loved the entire time by God, Who was looking for me to be born into a union of love, and I realized He had been my first love and my one, true love the entire time.

TRUE LOVE CAKE

Another amazing union to be happy about is this cake and your taste buds! Both are fundamental elements in the suitably named True Love Cake, a traditional cake at many weddings. This is my take on it, and the tenderness of the inside and tough edges on the outside remind me of the person I was back then.

1/2 cup butter
3/4 cup sugar
2 eggs
2 oz white chocolate
1 cup flour
1/8 tsp sea salt
2 1/2 tsp rosewater (you can use almond extract as a substitute if rosewater is hard to find or doesn't sound appealing)
powdered sugar (optional)

Preheat oven to 350. Melt the white chocolate in a small saucepan, keeping watch over it so that it doesn't scorch. Remove from heat as soon as the chocolate is melted. In a large bowl, beat the butter and sugar until the mixture becomes white. Add eggs one at a time and mix after each addition. Add flour, salt, and rosewater. Mix until smooth. Gently fold in the melted chocolate. Pour into prepared 8-inch square pan and bake for 30 to 35 minutes. Sprinkle with powdered sugar, if desired. (I desire!)

Serve this to any true loves in your life, or simply make it for yourself and know that you are loved!

LIGHTNING
Strikes

Have you ever said, "May lightning strike me if I'm lying?" Well, this story is the truth, but lightning struck me anyway.

I was seven months pregnant with Chelsea, skinning chicken at the kitchen sink. There was a garbage can to the side of me to catch the skins, a trickle of water from the faucet to wash the chicken pieces, and paper towels to set the meat on. Outside, it was pouring rain, thundering, and lightning.

Coincidentally, as I was standing there working the task at hand, my mind wandered to being a child and hearing the adults in my life telling me not to get in the shower during a storm. I even remember smiling and thinking how odd that was. I mean, lightning can't strike you inside! Old wives' tales—they can be silly.

Something—or Someone—was speaking to me, warning me. Alas, I ignored the warning. In the very next moment, I saw the brightest, whitest flash of light I had ever seen. There was no sound, as though there were the absence of sound altogether. It was a very peaceful moment, too, almost as if I were in a vacuum that closed in on me. The sound came a second later, as if the world had cracked in an explosion. My back hit the hallway wall behind me, knocking

11

out my breath. Then I slid to the floor. My body slunk down the wall after the hit, softly landing on my bum.

I kept saying, "I've been shot! I've been shot!" and looked for blood or obvious signs of impending death. Death by chicken skinning. I was a pioneer in the realm of stupid ways to die.

I couldn't move, though something was moving within me. Was that a bullet? Was it the phantom white light taking over my body? I looked up at the sink, which had broken, and saw black, sooty streaks over it, up the wall behind it, and on the counter surrounding it. The chicken had been blasted from its paper towel nest, which was now a wad of ashes.

Something moved inside me again. My arms, legs, face, and neck all felt tingly, as though they had fallen asleep. I couldn't move them.

Then it hit me: that movement was my baby, the baby I had been carrying for seven months, the baby I had waited for, the baby I had sworn to protect. I knew no matter what had happened, I needed to get to a doctor. This was back in the early 90s, y'all. Cellphones were not as prevalent as they are today. (Antiquated and old-fashioned, right, Young Readers?) But we made do.

I found the strength to pull myself back up the wall and over to the phone, body still quivering, tingling, and starting to feel as if I had walked through fire.

As I headed to the emergency room, I saw a small crowd outside my little apartment. They were standing in the drizzling rain, surrounding a large tree that had fallen and looked a lot like my sink did where it had broken.

It was that moment I somehow knew I had been struck by lightning. A few days later, I learned that lightning had, indeed, struck the tree outside, followed the path of least resistance through the ground, and had come through the faucet where I stood, skinning chicken and thinking about old wives' tales.

Luckily and obviously, I lived to tell about it. And so did that baby inside my belly, who, not ironically, has a very electric personality. (Sorry for the cheap joke. I couldn't help myself.) It did, however, put me on strict bedrest. I had dilated slightly and ran the risk of early labor. (I went two weeks over my due date, just for the record.)

Lightning strikes us in all kinds of ways. I speak with full authority as someone who has been struck not only by real lightning, but also as someone who, probably a lot like you, has faced the death of a loved one, the loss of jobs and finances, or the tragedy that makes you feel as though you can't move. But then something greater than yourself moved inside you.

I often think of that moment when I heard nothing and had that peculiar sense of peace, right before the explosion. Oh, there was a mess to clean up and bedrest to follow, but I always grabbed that peaceful instant that happened in the middle of the lightning strike for the reminder I needed to be freed from that misery.

Where can you find that peace when lightning strikes? Do you find yourself focusing on the explosion? Or do you reach for the peace, knowing and trusting you'll be OK one way or the other?

I now have a faith that I trust to take me through every proverbial lightning strike that happens, no matter how many trees it takes out in this path of life I'm on. But I no longer skin chicken when it's storming outside to invite the lightning in, either. Just so you know.

CRISPY SKINLESS FRIED CHICKEN FINGERS

juice of one lemon
4 eggs, beaten
2 1/2 cups sparkling water
4 lbs boneless, skinless chicken tenderloins
peanut oil
3 cups flour, halved
3 cups panko bread crumbs
2 tsp white pepper
1 tsp sea salt
3 tbs garlic powder
2 tsp rubbed sage

2 tbs dried parsley
2 tsp dried oregano
2 tsp dried thyme
1 tbs paprika
1/2 tsp cayenne

Pour peanut oil in a heavy pot (I use my cast-iron Dutch oven) and heat on medium heat until oil reaches about 350 degrees.* As your oil is heating, take a medium-sized bowl and mix lemon juice, eggs, sparkling water, 1 1/2 cups flour, 1 teaspoon sea salt, and 1/2 teaspoon white pepper.

In another medium-sized bowl, add remaining flour, panko bread crumbs, and remaining seasonings. Dredge your tenderloins in the dry-bowl ingredients, then the batter, and then the dry-bowl ingredients again. Place them on a baking rack or cooling rack as they each get done.

Carefully place four tenderloins into the hot oil and let fry for about 10 to 12 minutes, flipping them halfway through. Place cooked chicken fingers on a baking sheet or clean baking rack as you finish the remaining chicken tenderloins.

Every time I make these, I consider that I was struck by lightning. I stand over the stove and marvel at how much I've been through and how much more I can endure because of it. If you're feeling frisky, make these a little spicier and remember with every bite how lightning has struck you, too.

---

*If you do not have a cooking thermometer to check temperature of the oil, place the handle of a wooden spoon into the oil. If it sizzles around the handle, it is ready. Another method is to carefully drop one droplet of water into the oil. If it sizzles, it is ready. Also, fish out those cracklins with your slotted spoon as you cook. They are delicious!

MUSCLES
Don't Make the Man

When my second child, Cameron, was born, it was an easy birth. Don't get me wrong: it wasn't a breeze pushing out an eight-pound, three-ounce baby. But Chelsea had given me a run for my money, topping the clock at 13 hours of labor! Cameron took a mere six hours, and the contractions were somewhat easier. He was a beautiful boy, and he came out with a perfect, round head. (I must give credit to my friend, Sina, who helped me labor so that his head wouldn't be cone-shaped!) It wasn't long before his hair grew in curly, and his cheeks grew pink to enhance his olive skin.

But his life after birth wasn't so easy. It wasn't long before colic set in; that poor baby was often up for several nights in a row with it. Then there was the time Chelsea fed him coins. Though she was only 17 months old at the time, she was a quick little thing. From the time I put her in her car seat and buckled her in, said goodbye to my friend Jennifer, and got in, she had escaped her car seat, grabbed change from the console, and tried to "feed it" to her baby brother. He ended up having a penny surgically removed from his esophagus at only a month old.

As time progressed, so Cameron's struggles did too. He had childhood asthma that nearly took his life twice by the time he was two. The Children's Hospital was more of a home to him than where we lived. He was often sick, but his calm and sweet demeanor never wavered. He always, even at such a young age, tried to comfort *me*. He would put his chubby little hand in mine and smile, or wrap his arms around my neck and kiss me, or put my face in his hands and squish his nose against mine, looking me straight in the eyes. He was my inspiration. (Ugh. The tears—they flow again.)

Cameron was 11 when he was hit by an SUV while riding his bike. He had some broken bones and a bad concussion, but those weren't as bad as what else the X-rays found. There was a mass on his brain, his first Arachnoid cystic mass. It explained the horrible migraines he had been suffering from. Not long after, the second one was discovered, and then the pseudo-tumor on his spine was found. This kid was so sick.

You don't know how priceless life is until you've been told your child has five years at best to live. But Cameron stayed strong and never let anyone feel sorry for him, and now—way more than five years later—he is still here and not going anywhere fast. He chose to live every day as though it were his last because it should be like that for all of us, even if we're not sick. We watched him wake up in so much pain, sometimes throwing up from it, but brushing his teeth and moving forward, going to school or heading to baseball practice so he wouldn't let his team down.

Transverse myelitis set in from all the spinal taps Cameron needed. But he fought on. We looked into a balance between Western medicine and natural healing together as a team. During the time that Hurricane Rita unfurled around us, I remember watching Adrian carry Cameron, who was too sick and weak from a recent spinal tap to walk, to the living room gently to play board games by candlelight. Never once did Cameron ask, "Why me?" In fact, his faith increased as his health decreased.

A few years back, Cameron was in a car accident that nearly ended his life. Slight concussion, collapsed lung, four broken ribs, lacerated spleen, nearly-severed hand, fractured ankle. It was months of healing for him, along with the regular pain he had to deal with from the Arachnoids. But he stayed the course, with his integrity and character intact. After that incident, his car was totaled when a Ford Explorer slammed into the back of it at 60 miles per hour. Luckily, he wasn't inside of it at the time, but it was still another loss for him, just the same. Still he plows forward, doing everything he can to stay the course, have a good attitude, and keep the faith—a faith unlike anyone else's I've ever seen.

It's hard to keep a good attitude when you are constantly not feeling well or losing what you work hard for. But he manages. He is truly a faithful young man with a spirit of good fight in him. He is a rare human being in mind, body, and spirit. Not coincidentally, Cameron received his degree in Exercise Health and Science. He works out hard and keeps his body in good shape. It's his passion. He also has a passion for tattoos that express his love for the Lord. He loves his family so much, and he cares so deeply about what Adrian and I think, cautious to do his very best not to disappoint us. He still reaches for my hand or wraps his arms around me, still grabs my face, presses his nose into mine and looks me straight in the eyes to pick me up when I'm feeling down or scared or angry at the world—only now he's not the chubby little boy he once was. He is one of the strongest men I know. But we know that muscles don't make the man. Cameron's proof of that.

To see my son so sick and in pain manifested itself in my spirit, making me emotionally and spiritually sick and in pain. If I could have, I would have traded places with him so that he could be well. I cried myself to sleep, frustrated and wondering what the next day would hold for him. It was exhausting and taxing to my own faith. But to be reminded by my sick little boy that there is joy in this short life changed the way I see the world. To see him take it on as a great responsibility and honor was baffling and strengthening at the very same time. It grew me and it humbled me.

When the hard times come, it's easy to let them bring us down. When someone we know gets sick or dies, it's easy for us to get angry. When we lose our own health, it's easy for us to feel sorry for ourselves. When we don't have faith, we lose the will to live and to live well, regardless of the losses in our life.

Yes, the world changes when you have a child, especially if that child was made to help change it.

DRUNKEN MUSSELS

2 tbs butter
6 cloves garlic, minced
1 tsp red pepper flakes, or cayenne pepper
zest of one lemon
2 1/2 cups white wine
1/2 tsp sea salt
1 tbs pepper
1 tbs cumin
2 1/2 lbs mussels, cleaned and debearded
1 cup parsley, chopped coarsely

Melt butter in a large, heavy pot (I use my cast-iron Dutch oven) over medium heat. Add garlic and let cook for about one minute. Season with red pepper flakes (or cayenne, which has a more concentrated heat) and lemon zest, and stir. Pour in the wine and add seasonings. Bring to a boil and stir in mussels. Quickly cover the pot and, using your pot-holders to protect your hands, shake your pot for about ten seconds, and then let boil for about a minute. Stir mussels, and replace cover, letting it boil for about two more minutes until shells begin to open. Stir in parsley, cover pot again, and cook about three more minutes, until all shells are open.

NOTES: For a little acidity, squeeze some lemon over the mussels before serving. These are delicious on their own, but also taste fantastic with some crusty bread to soak up the juice.

Muscles don't make the man, but mussels definitely make the dinner!

CROSSING
Jordan

Being a blended family is no easy task, but it's been done since the dawn of time—remember Joseph?

Our blended family dynamic is one we are constantly and consistently working on. As people change and grow, so does the dynamic. I entered my marriage to Adrian with Chelsea and Cameron; Adrian came with Jordan, the youngest of the three. He has always been our quiet one. But, just like his dad, when he has something to say, it's funny, crazy, or profound.

I remember showing him how to tie his shoe: "Over, under, around, and through…that's how Jordan ties his shoe!" I remember him saying he wanted to be a fireman when he grew up, so I arranged for a tour of a firehouse. He screamed and cried the entire time, louder than the fire truck! Once, when he was about eight years old, he came home and said, "I've been thinking about what you were going to cook for dinner *all* day! You're a good cooker!"

Recently, he joined the Army, and as he stood there, a man swearing in to protect his country and our freedom, memories of that little boy ripped at my heart and made it swell with pride.

All good memories. I would be remiss if I told you it's all been cheese and lollipops though. Of course we've had disagreements. Of course we've had misunderstandings. Of course we've had moments of pain, suffering, and disappointment. We've had quite a few of those, actually. But doesn't that happen in every family?

What doesn't happen in every family—especially those rare, non-blended ones—are the pangs of jealousy from each respective parent's child—or even from the respective parent. Since we are being completely transparent here, of course there were whispered thoughts like, "Does he love his child more than me?" "Does he favor him over my children?" "He disciplines mine and not his." Oh, those are selfish-but-real moments of self-doubt and did-we-do-the-right-thing doubt. I look back on them now and realize they were all part of the growth process for us. I realize we are mere mortals in desperate search of love and family. I also realize how very far we've come.

I am grateful for Jordan. Without his even knowing it, he has changed my life in so many ways. Chelsea and Cameron are so outgoing and (booyah!) "in-yo-face." I've watched poor Jordan take a back seat to that so many times, but always with quiet fortitude and grace. I've learned from Jordan that you can scream something to someone in a relationship without ever making a sound and that sometimes that's best. I've also learned that you can love a child as though he is your very own. I've learned that a blood relation does not mean unconditional love, but rather that unconditional love deepens a relationship. I've learned that there are more than two sides to every story and that truth is vital.

I spend a lot of time writing about my family because they've all been strategically placed in my life to continue to form and mold me. I write about all the paths these people in my life have crossed and the way it's made me become She—the way it's helped me form my living legacy and the legacy I leave behind.

Who has made a difference in your life, who may not get quite the credit he or she deserves? Maya Angelou once said, "I've learned that people will forget what you said; people will forget what you did; but people will never forget how you made them feel."

HOT CROSS BUNS

1/2 cup apple juice
1/4 cup raisins
1/4 cup dried currants
1 1/4 cups milk
2 large eggs, plus one egg yolk (save the white for later)
6 tbs butter, softened
1 pkg fast-rising yeast
1/4 cup brown sugar, firmly packed
1 tbs ground cinnamon
1 tsp allspice
1 tsp ground nutmeg
2 tsp sea salt
1 tbs baking powder
4 1/2 cups flour

For the baste:
1 large egg white
2 tbs milk

For after they're baked:
4 tbs melted butter

Combine the raisins, currants, and apple juice in a small sauce pan and bring to a small boil, just until the fruit and liquid are very warm, and then remove from heat. Set aside to cool to room temperature. When the fruit mixture is cool, mix together all of the remaining ingredients except the milk and fruit. Heat the milk to just warm— don't boil it—and add to the dough mixture. Fold in the fruit and apple juice mixture. Let the dough rise for an hour, covered.

Using a greased ice cream scoop, form about 12 to 14 buns, and arrange them into a greased 9x13 pan. Cover the pan and let the buns rise for another hour, or until they've puffed up and are touching each other. Whisk together the reserved egg white and milk and brush it liberally over the buns. Bake the buns at 350 degrees for 20 minutes, until they're golden brown. Remove from the oven, baste with the melted butter, and transfer to a cooling rack.

NOTES: These are usually served with less-savory spices and with different types of dried fruits. It usually has a sweet cream cheese frosting drizzled over it in the shape of a cross—hence the name! I typically make them much more savory and skip the sweet frosting. I'm telling you, they are insanely good—like, *ridiculously* good.

Much like Jordan, these can be sweet or savory.

THE
Job Story

I am guessing that when you see "The Job Story," you might assume I mean the guy in the Bible who went through arguably the most difficult times ever documented, but came out on the other side restored, and then some, by God. It always strikes me as crazy that this is the man's legacy. Whenever anyone has a hard or difficult time, they say, "Well, consider Job," or "It could be worse. Think about what Job went through." I've even heard, "Your family has been through so much. It's like Job or something!"

Let me be the first to tell you: we have been through a lot, but nothing like that poor fella. And our faith, though strong, certainly doesn't match his, either, though we strive for that level of belief, devotion, and assurance every single day.

But when I say, "the job story," I am actually referring to a career. I mean all the jobs Adrian and I have lost over the years. I am referring to the tightening of our belts over and over, one lost job at a time.

It is very strange, the connection between The Hubster and me. When one is sick, the other has sympathy pains. When one is in the vicinity, the other can sense where. When one of us loses a job, we can almost be certain the other will too. This has not happened to us once, twice, or even three times, but many.

One could say it is the economy or a coincidence. It doesn't really matter why, does it? Rather than focus on the *why*'s, we needed to focus on feeding our baby birds and making certain we had running water and electricity.

We never really consider necessities and essentials as luxuries until we are in jeopardy of losing them, right? We turn the air conditioner down as low as it will go (we're in Texas, y'all) or fill the gas tank up without batting an eyelash. But let us lose our livelihood—especially at the same time as a spouse—and that means turning the air up and grabbing a fan, counting pennies for a few gallons of gas to get you to the next interview, fingers crossed.

We have always done what we had to do in order to survive, including pray, and we have never gone without. God has never let us down, and we truly believe He is not about to start now. Oh sure, that meant beans and rice nine-ways-to-Sunday and getting rid of cable television, but we were none the worse for wear and always came out restored on the other side.

I strongly believe it was always our little mustard seed of faith that moved the job mountains. I can't recall a time when we went hungry or didn't get the mortgage paid. Faith and our community (the two are harmonious to us) have always taken our lack of a job and somehow given us more. It made for hard times, certainly, but it also made for deeper trust and greater faith.

POOR MAN'S STEW

1 bag dry pinto beans
1 pkg smoked turkey sausage links or kielbasa, chopped into chunks
1 can Ro-tel
1 1/2 tbs sea salt
1 tbs pepper

2 tbs garlic powder

2 tbs cumin

1 tbs onion powder

1 tbs Penzey's Forward (or some other rich and flavorful spice in your cabinet)

4 bay leaves

This is easy. Watch this. Throw all ingredients into the crockpot, fill to the top of the pot with water, and set on low. Go on about your business. When it is done cooking, add a few more spices.* Serve over brown rice.

We've eaten this time and time again, and not once did anyone complain that we were having it again or that they were tired of it. I'm sure a lot of that had to do with how delicious it is, but more so, I believe it was that we were just happy to have it and to have it as a family.

---

*Crockpots tend to mute your seasoning, so it is always a good idea to season again to taste before you serve. Just be careful! You can always add, but you can never take away, and you don't want this to be too salty. (She said from experience.)

DRIVING

the Flames

You know the saying, "When it rains, it pours?" Well, that was where we were. Adrian (The Hubster) had recently lost his job, our air conditioner went kaput, and Cameron had been in an automobile accident that nearly ended his life, resulting in tons of rehabilitation, time spent away from my own job to help him do so, and unimaginable medical bills.

We were afraid to ask, "What next, Lord?" for fear He would show us. We certainly felt that each terrible event was just driving the flames higher for the next terrible event until we were singed beyond recognition.

Then one day, I was quite literally driving the flames.

I had just gotten Cameron set up in our big chair with an ottoman. His walker was by his side, his dinner in his lap, and his feet up. I had given him his medicine and placed his cell phone squarely beside him in case he needed me for anything.

I fed The Hubster the brandied onion soup he loves so much, cleaned up the dishes, and told him I was leaving for rehearsal with my band, The Texas Toast. Not only was rehearsal a great outlet for me, but it was also a way to help supplement our income with gigs, so I was not going to miss it.

A kiss for each of them and out the door I went.

As I was driving, I was also praying for strength and stamina. I told God that I trusted any and everything He allowed to happen to us and that I was sure there was a sovereign reason for it all. But as I was praying this, I became almost sure I smelled smoke. And where there's smoke, there's fire. I looked in my rearview mirror and all around me, but didn't see anything that would explain the smell. I assumed it was something outside or another car and went back to my prayers.

Pulling up to a red light, I heard several honks in the vicinity. "What a bunch of jerks," I thought to myself, mid-prayer. "Why do people feel the need to honk like that?" I looked in my rearview mirror once again to see what all the hubbub was about. It was then I saw the guy in the truck behind me waving frantically with both arms. Was he waving at me? I looked casually over to the car pulling up next to me on the right. The lady was also waving frantically.

It was then I saw the puffs of smoke coming between that car and mine. Still a little confused, I let my eyes follow it to its source, which led to a larger and larger amount of smoke coming from under my hood. My car seemed to be overheating.

Ah. There it was. The "next" thing to happen. Just what we needed. The light turned green, and I quickly looked for a safe place to park.

Only, as I began to drive again, flames began to lick my windshield. Flames! I reactively hit the brakes, only there were no brakes. I felt the pedal go all the way to the floor and the panic rise in my chest. The flames whipped out from either side of the hood and higher and higher up the windshield until I couldn't see. But I knew I couldn't just abandon the car where I was; it wasn't safe for other drivers or me.

"Lord, please help me!" I screamed it at the top of my lungs. I turned the steering wheel to the right, still pumping the brake pedal, as if it would magically come back. The car rolled down a little, bumped something gently, and came to a stop. I started to feel the heat in the driver's seat. I grabbed my phone and ran to the fast food restaurant directly in front of me.

I screamed for the guy behind the counter to call 9-1-1, telling him my car was on fire. The other guy next to him grabbed a fire extinguisher and headed out the door beside me. But there wasn't a fire extinguisher big enough to put this fire out. By this time, the flames had engulfed the car, and the entire front half was unrecognizable.

As I watched in horror, though, I also felt baffled at how the car was parked so perfectly between two yellow parking spot lines—though I hadn't been able to see through the flames. The tires had met the concrete bumper at the end of the parking spot, stopping the car.

As the fire engines screamed down the street, I called Adrian. What in the world was I going to say? I told him about the car and fire, of course, but what I remember most is the sound of my own brokenness, on my knees, tears hotter than those flames stinging my cheeks.

The car was totaled and we were only given a small percentage of what we had paid for it. To add insult to injury, this was the first brand new car I had ever owned, and it was only two years old. The investigation called the verdict for the fire "inconclusive." Now we were left without a car for Adrian to go on interviews or get Cameron to a doctor's visit since I had to get back-and-forth to work. Another notch in the I-don't-think-we-can-take-anymore belt.

But what I also took away from that experience was the memory of my husband and son pulling up in our truck, which was mysteriously running on empty, and watching my still-recuperating boy run with adrenaline through a ditch without his walker and with a cast on in order to get to me, still on my knees. I remember my amazing husband, my partner in life and for eternity—gently pulling me off my knees and wrapping his arms around me, saying, "We will be OK. We will get through this. All that matters is that you are safe, She. It could have been much worse."

And he was right.

Ironically, the story ends where it begins. We were still "finding trouble finding us," and still doing our best to remain faithful. We made our way home that night, exhausted, emotional, and spent. But the best memory I have is that we sat—together—and cried and prayed for a long time. And then we cried some more. Together. For a long time. When I think about that, I think about how all the things that drove the flames of one bad thing after another also drove the flames of standing together as a family and standing together in faith. I find beauty in those ashes.

I realize that I wouldn't trade one of those events leading up to that night, or any since. They forge the continued love and faith my family continues to find in this life we've been given, and they help us never take it for granted.

It's so easy to find glory in the good, but can you see purpose in the bad? What flames have driven you to a place of exhaustion and emotion? Search and find the good, and try to recall a good memory that may have occurred during the worst times. It will sometimes be the only way to extinguish the fire and find beauty for ashes.

BRANDIED ONION SOUP FLAMBE

This is no coincidence of a recipe. I actually have been making this for years for a comforting meal or to impress guests. I really do set it on fire, and I really did serve it to The Hubster that night.

6 red onions, peeled and sliced thinly
extra virgin olive oil (evoo)
1 cup brandy (or non-scotch whiskey), split
sea salt
pepper
2 boxes beef broth
cumin
garlic powder
1 baby brie, cut into small pieces
2 slices Swiss cheese, cut into medium-sized pieces

In a heavy soup pot,* sprinkle enough evoo to cover the bottom, and turn the stove to medium heat. Add onions and let sweat and brown for three minutes, stirring occasionally. Sprinkle the top with sea salt and pepper and stir. Using 1/2 cup of the brandy, add a little bit at a time, letting the onion cook and absorb the liquid. Each time the liquid is absorbed, add a little more until the entire 1/2 cup is used. Add the beef broth and sprinkle cumin and garlic powder to taste, adding a bit more sea salt and pepper. Cover and let simmer for fifteen minutes. Remove from heat and add brie and Swiss cheeses. Add rustic bread to bowl in chunks, if desired. Low carb? Leave out the bread! Once cooking is complete, remove from heat and pour remaining half cup of brandy on top of soup. Carefully light with a long match or lighter and let flames go down as the alcohol cooks out. Stir gently and serve.

This meal has become a staple in my house, whether it is just to have something cozy and relaxing, or because it is not expensive to make, and I usually have all the ingredients on hand. Either way, I get to control the flames from this fire!

---

*I use my cast-iron Dutch oven for this soup, and it works beautifully to help bring out the deep, rich flavor of the brandy and onions. If you want to impress your guests, ladle out soup into heat-safe bowls and split remaining brandy among bowls. Light each bowl individually or just light your entire pot of soup in the middle of the table as a centerpiece!

SKELETONS
and Bones

Many people probably picture a human skeleton when they think of skeletons and bones, or even a bone a dog might chew on. For me, I instantly think of the old adage, "Everyone has skeletons in the closet." It's true, you know? We all do.

Personally, I carry around quite a closet. I know that was a very frank statement, but most times I'm not brave enough to back it up by perhaps showing what's in it. Part of the entire Life As She Does It business—or persona, if you will—is to be an open book, and I am, for the most part. If you ask me a question, be certain you want the answer, because if you want the truth, I'm your gal; however, that doesn't mean I go around showing you all the old clothes that don't fit anymore in that proverbial closet, either.

Most people don't realize I'm extremely private. I love to take whatever pains me and sweep it under the rug. *Closets and rugs*—those phrases don't make themselves up. Instead of saying, "I've done things I'm not proud of," or "There are things going on in my life that embarrass me," we say, "Skeletons in the closet," and "Sweep it under the rug."

I come from a life of hard knocks. And I have fought very hard to put one foot in front of the other and make a better life for myself. Because of that, I've become the best "blocker-outer" you'll ever know. I am the queen of taking broken bones and patching them up just enough to get by and move forward, convincing myself that it's all part of the journey and that eventually they will straighten out on their own.

Some things from my past should be only for me, of course. Other things I use as testimony or way of helping others when the right time arises. Many things haunt me, whether they were the result of my own doing or someone else's.

But I have arrived at a precipice, a peak where I realize that each day comes bearing its own gifts, that the mind is owned by me but the heart is not. It belongs to all those I give it to, including those who break it.

I thought my broken relationships were increasing in speed at one point. I continued to be shattered over and over again with each significant relationship in my life—a friend, a relative, or otherwise. And so I never saw anything outside of them.

There was beauty in my life all around me. There were people fighting for me. There was joy to be had if only I would have it. Yet I kept stuffing those skeletons as high as they would be packed into that closet, as though joy were unattainable.

Those skeletons and bones gave me growth. They led me to my faith in Jesus. Those skeletons and bones made me the person I am today. They led me beyond the circumstances of who I thought I was supposed to be so that I could work out my salvation with fortitude and strive to be better each day.

I am now an ensemble of broken bones, skeletons, and hope. I wouldn't trade the things I've been through for anything. They've led me to a place of grace and mercy, and a place of understanding when it comes to others who are flawed and human as well. Those skeletons and bones give me wisdom. They give me the right perception of myself and others.

So what will you think of when you see the phrase "skeletons and bones" now? Hopefully, it will stir some things in you that you haven't thought about in a while, so that you remember where you came from, where you've arrived, and where you're headed.

Then, you can clean out your closet.

HAMBONE & BLACK BEAN SOUP

This is comforting and hearty. If the weather is cooling down, or it's a melancholy, rainy day, or if you're like me and you've considered the skeletons in your closet and could use some uplifting, make this your go-to!

1 pkg dry black beans, rinsed
2 large containers of beef broth (halved)
1 can of Ro-tel
1 small bone-in ham
1/4 cup red wine vinegar
1 large onion, chopped finely
4 garlic cloves, minced
1 bunch thyme, removed from stems
2 bay leaves
2 tbs Italian seasoning
2 tbs sea salt
1 tbs pepper

Throw all ingredients into a crockpot, cook low-and-slow for about 6–8 hours. Pour in additional broth as needed. When it's done, remove bay leaves and ham bone. Shred the ham with two forks, slice with a knife and fork, or just chunk it up. Add back to soup and re-season if necessary, since sometimes a crockpot can mute your flavors. Enjoy with crusty, chewy bread.

Stay the course of conquering this one life we've been given. And no matter what it brings you, through some experience, lots of faith, and tons of food, I pray you find the inspiration to move forward and be comforted.

Epilogue

I n my past blog posts and books, this book, and the books to come, my hope and prayer is that when there are hard times, you realize there is still joy and comfort to be found. These were only a few of the stories from a lifetime of sickness, loss, battles, and bruises. And they were only a few of the many times God revealed Himself to me in a way that helped me see the light through the darkness.

These are things we've all been through and will continue to go through, because such is life. We can choose to live with bitter hearts and waste whatever time we have left, or we can choose to build our legacy in a way that will make a difference in the lives of those around us.

I've always wondered why I was given the gift of cooking and creating wonderful meals from the food that fuels us. I mean, really? Cooking as a gift? And how could I possibly incorporate that into my own legacy? But I am now able to see how often we use food as our go-to for everything that happens to us, and how I can show my love language through healthy and delicious food while also showing my healthy and delicious faith.

We will talk again soon, You Lovely Souls.

CPSIA information can be obtained
at www.ICGtesting.com
Printed in the USA
BVHW04*1453191018
530215BV00008B/1105/P